SMART BRAIN RIGHT BRAIN

An Introduction to Computer Technology

Om KIDZ
An imprint of Om Books International

First Published in 2021 by

Om KIDZ | Om Books International

Corporate & Editorial Office
A-12, Sector 64, Noida 201 301
Uttar Pradesh, India
Phone: +91 120 477 4100
Email: editorial@ombooks.com
Website: www.ombooksinternational.com

Sales Office
107, Ansari Road, Darya Ganj
New Delhi 110 002, India
Phone: +91 11 4000 9000
Email: sales@ombooks.com
Website: www.ombooks.com

Author: Shweta Sinha
Editor: Kirti Pathak
Art & Design: Anshuman Pandey, Gaurav Bhandari, Harish Arya

ISBN: 978-93-5276-837-0

Printed in India

10 9 8 7 6 5 4 3 2 1

CONTENTS

1. What Is a Computer?

Amy's Mom is buying a new computer. Amy's Mom needs the computer for her official work. But Amy can play games on it too. What is a computer, anyway?

POCKET FACT

Charles Babbage invented the first computer in 1833.

A computer is an electronic machine. A computer can be of many types. It can be as big as a room, or smaller than a banana. Amy's Mom probably wants to buy a personal computer.

A personal computer can be:

- a desktop computer.
- a laptop.
- a tablet.

POCKET FACT

A smartphone is a type of computer too.

A computer for everyone

Can you find a computer in these pictures?

Did you find any computer in the pictures?

- A car has a navigation system. The navigation system is a computer.
- The dog is wearing a tracking collar. That collar is a computer.
- A washing machine has a panel to set the wash program. The panel is a computer.
- A supermarket is full of many types of computers—cashier machines, burglar alarms, price scanners, and many more.

POCKET FACT

A supercomputer is a really powerful computer. It can be 1,000 times faster than the computer you use at home.

2. Why Do We Need a Computer?

It's simple. A computer makes our work easier.

A computer is really fast and accurate

A computer has something called a microprocessor inside it. The microprocessor lets a computer solve problems in a jiffy. A computer always computes the correct results.

A computer never gets tired

It can keep working all day without rest. For example, you may get tired, but the computer in a smart watch won't.

A computer remembers everything

A computer has a great memory. It can save tons of information, like photos, videos, documents, songs, and much, much more.

A computer helps us connect with others

You can search for information on the internet. You can send an email anywhere in the world. You can even see your friends on video chat.

3. How Does a Computer Work?

Computers are smart, but only as smart as their software. They do nothing unless you tell them what to do. A software is a set of instructions you give the computer. It instructs the computer to do a task. There are software to draw. And another to play games. There are also software to send emails, or to listen to music.

DID YOU KNOW?

A software on a smartphone is called an 'app'.

What if a computer had hands and you wanted it to make you a sandwich?

This is how you would have to instruct the computer:

1. Open a packet of bread.
2. Take out two slices.
3. Open the jar of peanut butter.
4. Use a knife to spread some peanut butter on the slices.
5. Close the jar.
6. Stick the two slices together.

A software program is pretty much like this recipe.

Ta-da... your sandwich is ready.

POCKET FACT

You cannot point towards or touch a software.

4. Hardware and Software

The parts of a computer that you can see and touch are called 'hardware'.

So, a computer = hardware + software.

The hardware includes all the physical parts of a computer. The monitor, keyboard, printer and mouse are hardware.

The software are all the programs that run inside a computer. Video games, Notepad and Paint are software.

POCKET FACT

A computer gets heated up while working. So, it has a fan to keep it cool.

Which of these pictures are a part of a computer?

	or	
	or	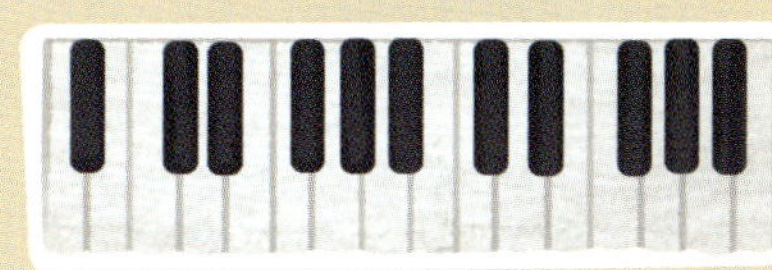
	or	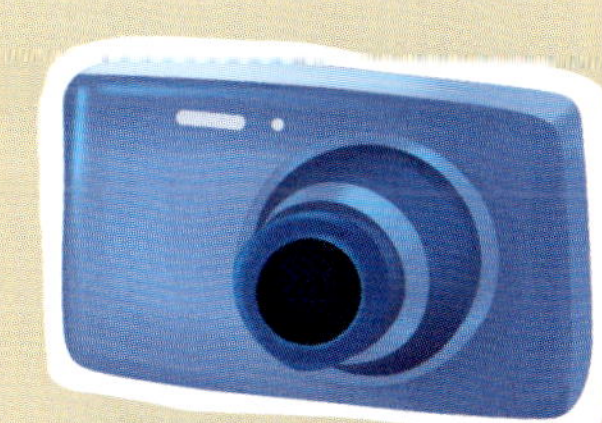
	or	
	or	
	or	

5. What Are the Basic Parts of a Computer?

Look at this desktop computer. How many parts can you see? Can you name them all?

DID YOU KNOW? Wires and cables are used to connect the different parts of the computer.

Different parts of a computer have different jobs to perform.

- Some parts send information to the computer. They are called **input devices**. The mouse, keyboard and microphone are input devices.

- Some parts take data from a computer. They are called the **output devices**. The monitor, printer and speaker are output devices.

- Some parts save information. They are called the **storage devices**. The hard drive, pen drive, CD and SD cards are storage devices.

DID YOU KNOW?

The first computer mouse in the world was made of wood.

Computer Tower/CPU

This is the box that does the main work. It is the brain of the computer.

Keyboard

A keyboard has lots of keys. Each key stands for a letter, number or a symbol. You type using a keyboard.

Mouse

The mouse is a pointing device. It lets you click, drag, select and point with the little arrow on the monitor.

Monitor

This is the place where you see all the images. A monitor looks like a TV screen. It shows you whatever you type with a keyboard or draw with a mouse.

Microphone

It lets you input sounds into the computer. You can record your voice using a microphone.

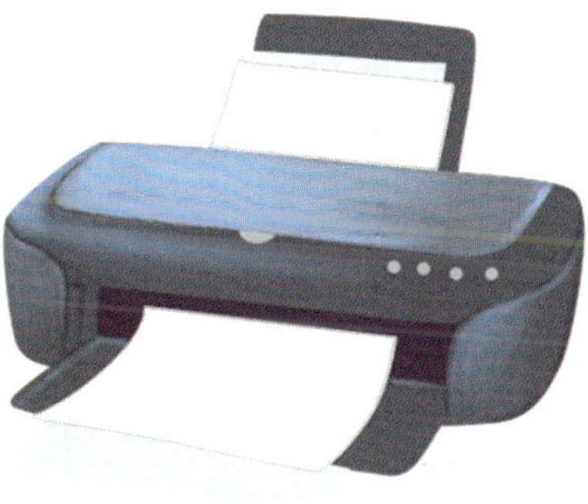

Printer

If you want to print what you see on the monitor, use a printer. The printed paper is called a 'printout'. A printer is an output device.

Speaker

Speakers are output devices to hear songs and sounds. Headphones are like speakers, but only one person can listen on it. You can use headphones when you don't want to disturb others.

POCKET FACT

A printout is also called a 'Hard Copy'. Something saved on the computer is a 'Soft Copy'.

6. Input, Output and Processing

What happens when you type your name on a computer? You type the letters on the keyboard and see them on the screen. What did the computer do?

The real work takes place inside the computer. The computer 'processes' the input data from the input device. It reads the instructions and decides what to do. Then the computer sends the results to the output device. When you press a key, the computer tells the monitor to display it. All of this happens faster than you blink.

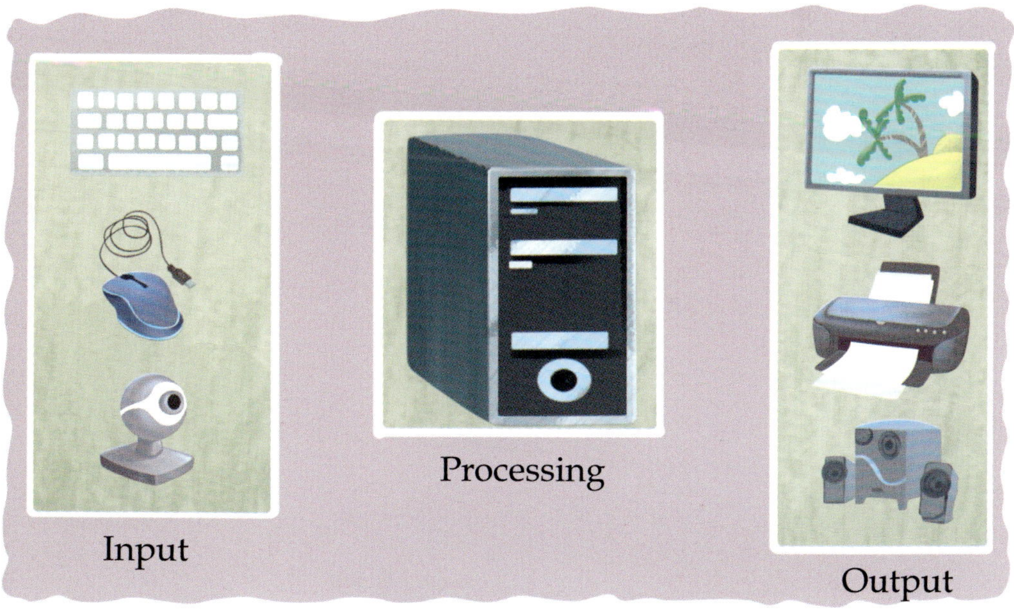

DID YOU KNOW? All the wires and circuits inside the main computer box are also 'Hardware'.

What is 'Processing'?

If you wanted to watch a movie, what will you need?

You need to play the DVD in a DVD player. That is Processing.

Where else do you 'process' an input to get an output?

Input	Action/Processing	Output
Clay 	Shape the clay with your hands 	A flower 
Banana, milk, sugar, ice 	Blend all in a blender 	Banana Shake 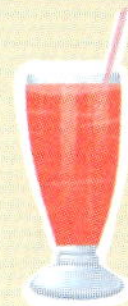
Numbers 5 and 10	Add (5+10)	15
Pencils, paints, paper 	Draw and paint a picture on paper 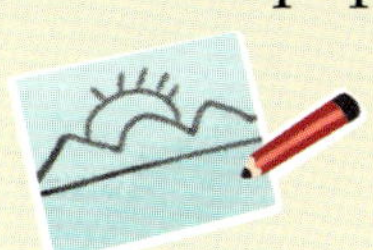	A painting 

DID YOU KNOW?

Processing is done by software programs inside the computer.

7. A Peek Inside a Computer

Inside the computer tower are circuit boards. On the main circuit board you will find the CPU. CPU stands for Central Processing Unit. The CPU is a bit bossy. It tells the other parts what to do. Its job is to carry out your commands.

POCKET FACT

The CPU is called the brain of the computer.

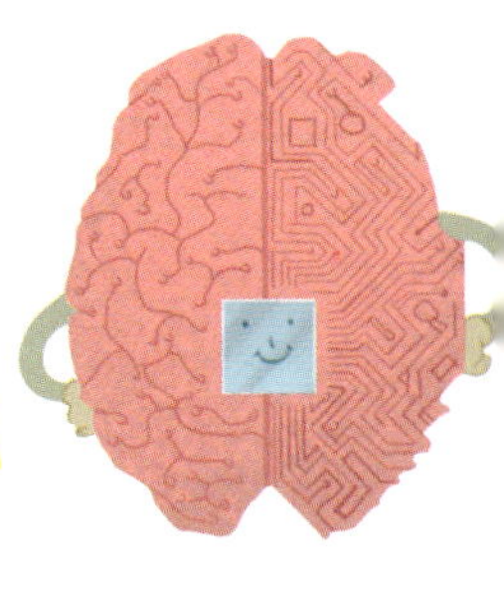

Then there are the helpful RAM and ROM. They help the CPU to remember things. Together, they are called 'Memory'. But they cannot remember things for too long.

The Hard Drive is really big-hearted. It lets you save information for as long as you want.

DID YOU KNOW?

Early hard disks weighed more than 200 kg. That is heavier than a gorilla!

8. Do's and Don'ts Around a Computer

Remember:

This is a bad posture.

This is the correct way to sit:

Touch your computer with gentle hands

Be gentle when using the keyboard, mouse or headphones. Some computers have a touchscreen. A smartphone and a tab have touchscreens too. A touchscreen is super delicate. It can easily crack and break! Be gentle with your touchscreen.

DID YOU KNOW?

Spilling food or liquid on a computer can damage its inside parts.

How to look after your computer

- Keep your computer clean. Don't use sprays to clean your computer. Use only a lint cloth.
- Never spill food or drinks on a computer.
- Don't insert your finger, a pencil or any such thing inside a computer.
- Never pull out wires from a computer. Computers runs on electricity. Playing with wires can be dangerous for you. If you find any hanging wire, tell a grownup.

- Do not install programs without permission.
- Switch off the computer when you are done.

POCKET FACT

Just as a virus makes you fall sick, computer viruses also cause computers to stop working.

Computer Parts

Find these words in the grid.

COMPUTER	HARDWARE	SOFTWARE	KEYBOARD
MOUSE	PRINTER	SPEAKER	MEMORY

M	K	B	P	P	R	I	N	T	E	R
W	Z	C	S	I	V	B	T	S	O	A
S	O	F	T	W	A	R	E	P	O	Z
Q	C	X	F	I	Y	M	L	E	K	H
K	O	G	G	O	X	Y	F	A	Z	A
D	M	U	R	M	A	S	U	K	K	R
T	P	Z	E	A	H	G	O	E	I	D
X	U	K	A	M	E	M	O	R	Y	W
D	T	E	L	Z	M	O	U	S	E	A
K	E	Y	B	O	A	R	D	K	S	R
G	R	T	B	Q	W	A	W	S	C	E

Match the name of the correct parts of the computer to the picture.

Headphones

Computer Tower

Keyboard

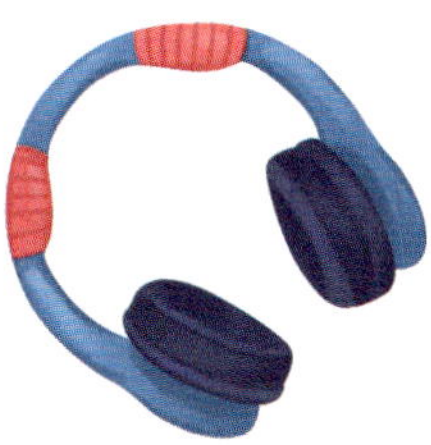

Monitor

Printer

Input, Output and Storage

Guess the type of device and tick the correct box.

	Input Device	Output Device	Storage Device
Speakers 			
Microphone 			
Pen Drive 			
Mouse 			
Hard Drive 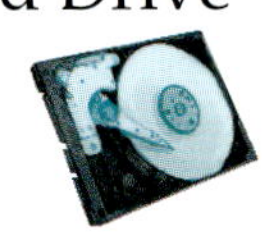			
Webcam 			
Printer 			

Software or Hardware

Connect the pictures to correct box.

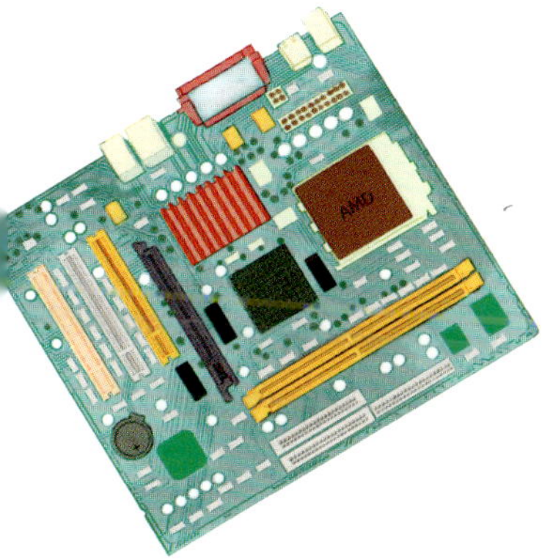

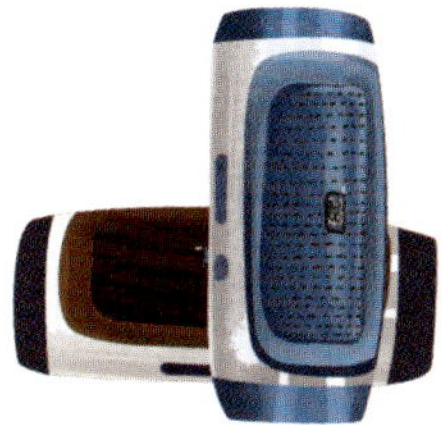

HARDWARE

SOFTWARE

GLOSSARY

Abacus	counting device made from beads and string
Circuit board	a plastic board made for connecting electronic components together
Commands	a line of code or instruction sent to a computer
Data	any information stored by a computer. It can be files, e-mails, video games, songs, pictures, etc.
Desktop computer	the type of computer you have at home with the monitor and computer connected
Information	news or knowledge received or given
Internet	many computers that are connected like a web so you can see what other computer operators show you and you can show them things as well
Laptop	a small portable computer
Memory	the data that a computer stores
Navigation system	a GPS-based electronic system in a vehicle or mobile device
Posture	the position of a body while standing or sitting
Virus	software that was written to do bad stuff to your computer

ANSWERS

Page 28.

M	K	B	P	P	R	I	N	T	E	R
W	Z	C	S	I	V	B	T	S	O	A
S	O	F	T	W	A	R	E	P	O	Z
Q	C	X	F	I	Y	M	L	E	K	H
K	O	G	G	O	X	Y	F	A	Z	A
D	M	U	R	M	A	S	U	K	K	R
T	P	Z	E	A	H	G	O	E	I	D
X	U	K	A	M	E	M	O	R	Y	W
D	T	E	L	Z	M	O	U	S	E	A
K	E	Y	B	O	A	R	D	K	S	R
G	R	T	B	Q	W	A	W	S	C	E

Page 29.

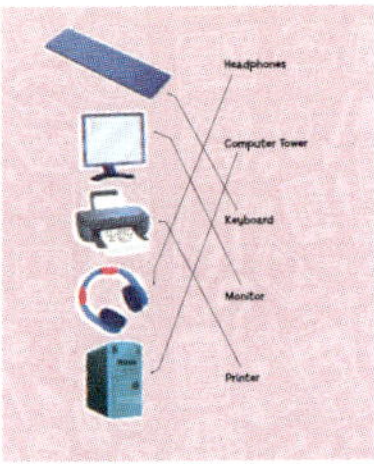

Page 30. Input devices - Microphone, Mouse, Webcam
Output devices - Speaker, Printer
Storage devices - Pen Drive, Hard Drive

Page 31.